GOD'S
PROMISES
OF
Provision

BENNY HINN

Scripture quotations are from the
KING JAMES VERSION

ISBN #
1-881256-29-4

Introduction

The Bible is filled with God's promises of blessing for His children . . . promises that extend into every area of life. God's love for His children and His willingness to bless those who love and honor Him are clearly illustrated in His dealings with the Children of Israel. His faithfulness to them year after year, extended into every aspect of their lives. And the promises of God to the Children of Israel found throughout scripture are extended to you and me today as His children.

These promises belong to every believer. When we walk in the ways of the Lord, when we live according to God's principles and meet the conditions outlined throughout the Word of God, God promises to pour out blessings in such abundance that we cannot contain them. Malachi 3:10 states, ". . . and prove me now herewith, saith the Lord of hosts, if I will not open you the windows of heaven, and pour you out a blessing, that there shall not be room enough to receive it."

God wants to bless His obedient children far more

than we can even comprehend. The Apostle Paul hints at this when he declares, "Eye hath not seen, nor ear heard, neither have entered into the heart of man, the things which God hath prepared for them that love him" (1 Corinthians 2:9). In some ways this verse is the key: God has prepared so much for those who love Him.

Experiencing the incredible life of blessing that God has for you really isn't any more complicated than falling in love with the Almighty, and allowing Him to do all for you that He intends. The life of blessing that He has in store for you as His child isn't found in formulas and techniques. It's simply falling in love with God the Father. And as in any relationship between a good father and an obedient child, the child moves in love and trust with his father, and the father pours the best into the life of that child, giving the child the things he needs each day, and at times joyfully showering him with good things that just bring pleasure to the child.

His Promises Are True

The report of King Solomon to the assembly of Israel is just as true today as it was when he delivered it so long ago, declaring in 1 Kings 8:56, "Blessed be the Lord, that hath given rest unto his people Israel, according to all that he promised: there hath not failed one word of all his good promise, which he promised by the hand of Moses his servant."

God's promises have no expiration date! They are as true today as they were when they were first spoken and recorded. And they are available to you and me!

The following pages contain many of the scriptures which deal with blessings that are promised to the believer. Many of these scriptures are favorites of mine and have been a blessing to me personally.

Some individuals mistakenly connect the word "blessings" only to finances, and although that is included in God's promises to His children, it is just one of the many areas of our lives in which God blesses.

God has blessed me in so many ways, and the blessings I have experienced in my life, my family, my ministry and in my walk with God are beyond anything I ever dreamed possible. And you can know the joy and fulfillment of this life of blessing, too.

Promised Blessings

Throughout Scripture we find many references to God's willingness and earnest desire to bless His children. The verses included in this book represent but a small portion of the many promises contained in the Word of God.

I have chosen to share a few of these scriptures to help you understand just how much God wants to bless His children in every area of life: both in the natural realm and the spiritual realm. And as a believer, these blessings are promised to you and your children. Claim them in prayer and expect to be blessed abundantly.

Benny Hinn

GENESIS
Genesis 1:26-28

26 And God said, Let us make man in our image, after our likeness: and let them have dominion over the fish of the sea, and over the fowl of the air, and over the cattle, and over all the earth, and over every creeping thing that creepeth upon the earth.

27 So God created man in his own image, in the image of God created he him; male and female created he them.

28 And God blessed them, and God said unto them, Be fruitful, and multiply, and replenish the earth, and subdue it: and have dominion over the fish of the sea, and over the fowl of the air, and over every living thing that moveth upon the earth.

Genesis 22:15-17

15 And the angel of the Lord called unto Abraham out of heaven the second time.

16 And said, By myself have I sworn, saith the Lord, for because thou hast done this thing, and hast

not withheld thy son, thine only son:

17 That in blessing I will bless thee, and in multiplying I will multiply thy seed as the stars of the heaven, and as the sand which is upon the sea shore; and thy seed shall possess the gate of his enemies;

EXODUS
Exodus 12:36

36 And the Lord gave the people favour in the sight of the Egyptians, so that they lent unto them such things as they required. And they spoiled the Egyptians.

LEVITICUS
Leviticus 26:3-9

3 If ye walk in my statutes, and keep my commandments, and do them;

4 Then I will give you rain in due season, and the land shall yield her increase, and the trees of the field shall yield their fruit.

5 And your threshing shall reach unto the vintage, and the vintage shall reach unto the sowing time: and ye shall eat your bread to the full, and dwell in your land safely.

6 And I will give peace in the land, and ye shall lie down, and none shall make you afraid: and I will rid evil beasts out of the land, neither shall the sword go through your land.

7 And ye shall chase your enemies, and they shall fall before you by the sword.

8 And five of you shall chase an hundred, and an

hundred of you shall put ten thousand to flight: and your enemies shall fall before you by the sword.

9 For I will have respect unto you, and make you fruitful, and multiply you, and establish my covenant with you.

NUMBERS
Numbers 6:22-27

22 And the Lord spake unto Moses, saying,

23 Speak unto Aaron and unto his sons, saying, On this wise ye shall bless the children of Israel, saying unto them,

24 The Lord bless thee, and keep thee:

25 The Lord make his face shine upon thee, and be gracious unto thee:

26 The Lord lift up his countenance upon thee, and give thee peace.

27 And they shall put my name upon the children of Israel; and I will bless them.

DEUTERONOMY
Deuteronomy 8:18

18 But thou shalt remember the Lord thy God: for it is he that giveth thee power to get wealth, that he may establish his covenant which he sware unto thy fathers, as it is this day.

Deuteronomy 14:22-23

22 Thou shalt truly tithe all the increase of thy seed, that the field bringeth forth year by year.

23 And thou shalt eat before the Lord thy God, in

the place which he shall choose to place his name there, the tithe of thy corn, of thy wine, and of thine oil, and the firstlings of thy herds and of thy flocks; that thou mayest learn to fear the Lord thy God always.

Deuteronomy 26:1, 2, 18, 19

1 And it shall be, when thou art come in unto the land which the Lord thy God giveth thee for an inheritance, and possessest it, and dwellest therein;

2 That thou shalt take of the first of all the fruit of the earth, which thou shalt bring of thy land that the Lord thy God giveth thee, and shalt put it in a basket, and shalt go unto the place which the Lord thy God shall choose to place his name there.

18 And the Lord hath avouched thee this day to be his peculiar people, as he hath promised thee, and that thou shouldest keep all his commandments;

19 And to make thee high above all nations which he hath made, in praise, and in name, and in honour; and that thou mayest be an holy people unto the Lord thy God, as he hath spoken.

Deuteronomy 28:1-13

1 And it shall come to pass, if thou shalt hearken diligently unto the voice of the Lord thy God, to observe and to do all his commandments which I command thee this day, that the Lord thy God will set thee on high above all nations of the earth:

2 And all these blessings shall come on thee, and overtake thee, if thou shalt hearken unto the voice of the Lord thy God.

3 Blessed shalt thou be in the city, and blessed shalt thou be in the field.

4 Blessed shall be the fruit of thy body, and the fruit of thy ground, and the fruit of thy cattle, the increase of thy kine, and the flocks of thy sheep.

5 Blessed shall be thy basket and thy store.

6 Blessed shalt thou be when thou comest in, and blessed shalt thou be when thou goest out.

7 The Lord shall cause thine enemies that rise up against thee to be smitten before thy face: they shall come out against thee one way, and flee before thee seven ways.

8 The Lord shall command the blessing upon thee in thy storehouses, and in all that thou settest thine hand unto; and he shall bless thee in the land which the Lord thy God giveth thee.

9 The Lord shall establish thee an holy people unto himself, as he hath sworn unto thee, if thou shalt keep the commandments of the Lord thy God, and walk in his ways.

10 And all people of the earth shall see that thou art called by the name of the Lord; and they shall be afraid of thee.

11 And the Lord shall make thee plenteous in goods, in the fruit of thy body, and in the fruit of thy cattle, and in the fruit of thy ground, in the land which the Lord sware unto thy fathers to give thee.

12 The Lord shall open unto thee his good treasure, the heaven to give the rain unto thy land in his season, and to bless all the work of thine hand: and thou shalt lend unto many nations, and thou shalt not borrow.

13 And the Lord shall make thee the head, and not the tail; and thou shalt be above only, and thou shalt not be beneath; if that thou hearken unto the commandments of the Lord thy God, which I command thee this day, to observe and to do them:

Deuteronomy 33:27

27 The eternal God is thy refuge, and underneath are the everlasting arms: and he shall thrust out the enemy from before thee; and shall say, Destroy them.

JOSHUA
Joshua 1:8

8 This book of the law shall not depart out of thy mouth; but thou shalt meditate therein day and night, that thou mayest observe to do according to all that is written therein: for then thou shalt make thy way prosperous, and then thou shalt have good success.

JUDGES
Judges 5:12, 13

12 Awake, awake, Deborah: awake, awake, utter a song: arise, Barak, and lead thy captivity captive, thou son of Abinoam.

13 Then he made him that remaineth have dominion over the nobles among the people: the Lord made me have dominion over the mighty.

RUTH
Ruth 4:15

15 And he shall be unto thee a restorer of thy life, and a nourisher of thine old age: for thy daughter in law, which loveth thee, which is better to thee than seven sons, hath borne him.

1 SAMUEL
1 Samuel 2:27-30

27 And there came a man of God unto Eli, and said unto him, Thus saith the Lord, Did I plainly appear unto the house of thy father, when they were in Egypt in Pharaohs house?

28 And did I choose him out of all the tribes of Israel to be my priest, to offer upon mine altar, to burn incense, to wear an ephod before me? and did I give unto the house of thy father all the offerings made by fire of the children of Israel?

29 Wherefore kick ye at my sacrifice and at mine offering, which I have commanded in my habitation; and honourest thy sons above me, to make yourselves fat with the chiefest of all the offerings of Israel my people?

30 Wherefore the Lord God of Israel saith, I said indeed that thy house, and the house of thy father, should walk before me for ever: but now the Lord saith, Be it far from me; for them that honour me I will honour, and they that despise me shall be lightly esteemed.

2 SAMUEL
2 Samuel 22:17-20; 29-37

17 He sent from above, he took me; he drew me out of many waters:

18 He delivered me from my strong enemy, and from them that hated me: for they were too strong for me.

19 They prevented me in the day of my calamity: but the Lord was my stay.

20 He brought me forth also into a large place: he delivered me, because he delighted in me.

29 For thou art my lamp, O Lord: and the Lord will lighten my darkness.

30 For by thee I have run through a troop: by my God have I leaped over a wall.

31 As for God, his way is perfect; the word of the Lord is tried: he is a buckler to all them that trust in him.

32 For who is God, save the Lord? and who is a rock, save our God?

33 God is my strength and power: and he maketh my way perfect.

34 He maketh my feet like hinds' feet: and setteth me upon my high places.

35 He teacheth my hands to war; so that a bow of steel is broken by mine arms.

36 Thou hast also given me the shield of thy salvation: and thy gentleness hath made me great.

37 Thou hast enlarged my steps under me; so that my feet did not slip.

1 KINGS
1 Kings 2:1-3

1 Now the days of David drew nigh that he should die; and he charged Solomon his son, saying,

2 I go the way of all the earth: be thou strong therefore, and shew thyself a man;

3 And keep the charge of the Lord thy God, to walk in his ways, to keep his statutes, and his commandments, and his judgments, and his testimonies, as it is written in the law of Moses, that thou mayest prosper in all that thou doest, and whithersoever thou turnest thyself:

1 Kings 8:56

56 Blessed be the Lord, that hath given rest unto his people Israel, according to all that he promised: there hath not failed one word of all his good promise, which he promised by the hand of Moses his servant.

1 Kings 17:10-16

10 So he arose and went to Zarephath. And when he came to the gate of the city, behold, the widow woman was there gathering of sticks: and he called to her, and said, Fetch me, I pray thee, a little water in a vessel, that I may drink.

11 And as she was going to fetch it, he called to her, and said, Bring me, I pray thee, a morsel of bread in thine hand.

12 And she said, As the Lord thy God liveth, I have not a cake, but an handful of meal in a barrel, and a little oil in a cruse: and, behold, I am gathering two

sticks, that I may go in and dress it for me and my son, that we may eat it, and die.

13 And Elijah said unto her, Fear not; go and do as thou hast said: but make me thereof a little cake first, and bring it unto me, and after make for thee and for thy son.

14 For thus saith the Lord God of Israel, The barrel of meal shall not waste, neither shall the cruse of oil fail, until the day that the Lord sendeth rain upon the earth.

15 And she went and did according to the saying of Elijah: and she, and he, and her house, did eat many days.

16 And the barrel of meal wasted not, neither did the cruse of oil fail, according to the word of the Lord, which he spake by Elijah.

2 KINGS

2 Kings 4:1-7

1 Now there cried a certain woman of the wives of the sons of the prophets unto Elisha, saying, Thy servant my husband is dead; and thou knowest that thy servant did fear the Lord: and the creditor is come to take unto him my two sons to be bondmen.

2 And Elisha said unto her, What shall I do for thee? tell me, what hast thou in the house? And she said, Thine handmaid hath not any thing in the house, save a pot of oil.

3 Then he said, Go, borrow thee vessels abroad of all thy neighbours, even empty vessels; borrow not a few.

4 And when thou art come in, thou shalt shut the door upon thee and upon thy sons, and shalt pour out into all those vessels, and thou shalt set aside that which is full.

5 So she went from him, and shut the door upon her and upon her sons, who brought the vessels to her; and she poured out.

6 And it came to pass, when the vessels were full, that she said unto her son, Bring me yet a vessel. And he said unto her, There is not a vessel more. And the oil stayed.

7 Then she came and told the man of God. And he said, Go, sell the oil, and pay thy debt, and live thou and thy children of the rest.

1 CHRONICLES
1 Chronicles 29:10-13

10 Wherefore David blessed the Lord before all the congregation: and David said, Blessed be thou, Lord God of Israel our father, for ever and ever.

11 Thine, O Lord is the greatness, and the power, and the glory, and the victory, and the majesty: for all that is in the heaven and in the earth is thine; thine is the kingdom, O Lord, and thou art exalted as head above all.

12 Both riches and honour come of thee, and thou reignest over all; and in thine hand is power and might; and in thine hand it is to make great, and to give strength unto all.

13 Now therefore, our God, we thank thee, and praise thy glorious name.

2 CHRONICLES
2 Chronicles 20:22-27

22 And when they began to sing and to praise, the Lord set ambushments against the children of Ammon, Moab, and mount Seir, which were come against Judah; and they were smitten.

23 For the children of Ammon and Moab stood up against the inhabitants of mount Seir, utterly to slay and destroy them: and when they had made an end of the inhabitants of Seir, every one helped to destroy another.

24 And when Judah came toward the watch tower in the wilderness, they looked unto the multitude, and, behold, they were dead bodies fallen to the earth, and none escaped.

25 And when Jehoshaphat and his people came to take away the spoil of them, they found among them in abundance both riches with the dead bodies, and precious jewels, which they stripped off for themselves, more than they could carry away: and they were three days in gathering of the spoil, it was so much.

26 And on the fourth day they assembled themselves in the valley of Berachah; for there they blessed the Lord: therefore the name of the same place was called, The valley of Berachah, unto this day.

27 Then they returned, every man of Judah and Jerusalem, and Jehoshaphat in the forefront of them, to go again to Jerusalem with joy; for the Lord had made them to rejoice over their enemies.

2 Chronicles 26:5

5 And he sought God in the days of Zechariah, who had understanding in the visions of God: and as long as he sought the Lord, God made him to prosper.

EZRA
Ezra 8:22b-23

22b The hand of our God is upon all them for good that seek him; but his power and his wrath is against all them that forsake him.

23 So we fasted and besought our God for this: and he was intreated of us.

NEHEMIAH
Nehemiah 5:1-4; 11, 12

1 And there was a great cry of the people and of their wives against their brethren the Jews.

2 For there were that said, We, our sons, and our daughters, are many: therefore we take up corn for them, that we may eat, and live.

3 Some also there were that said, We have mortgaged our lands, vineyards, and houses, that we might buy corn, because of the dearth.

4 There were also that said, We have borrowed money for the king's tribute, and that upon our lands and vineyards.

11 Restore, I pray you, to them, even this day, their lands, their vineyards, their oliveyards, and their houses, also the hundredth part of the money, and of the corn, the wine, and the oil, that ye exact of them.

12 Then said they, We will restore them, and will require nothing of them; so will we do as thou sayest. Then I called the priests, and took an oath of them, that they should do according to this promise.

ESTHER
Esther 2:15b
15b And Esther obtained favour in the sight of all them that looked upon her.

JOB
Job 5:19-22
19 He shall deliver thee in six troubles: yea, in seven there shall no evil touch thee.

20 In famine he shall redeem thee from death: and in war from the power of the sword.

21 Thou shalt be hid from the scourge of the tongue: neither shalt thou be afraid of destruction when it cometh.

22 At destruction and famine thou shalt laugh: neither shalt thou be afraid of the beasts of the earth.

Job 8:7
7 Though thy beginning was small, yet thy latter end should greatly increase.

Job 8:20-22
20 Behold, God will not cast away a perfect man, neither will he help the evil doers:

21 Till he fill thy mouth with laughing, and thy lips with rejoicing.

22 They that hate thee shall be clothed with shame; and the dwelling place of the wicked shall come to nought.

Job 22:21-28

21 Acquaint now thyself with him, and be at peace: thereby good shall come unto thee.

22 Receive, I pray thee, the law from his mouth, and lay up his words in thine heart.

23 If thou return to the Almighty, thou shalt be built up, thou shalt put away iniquity far from thy tabernacles.

24 Then shalt thou lay up gold as dust, and the gold of Ophir as the stones of the brooks.

25 Yea, the Almighty shall be thy defense, and thou shalt have plenty of silver.

26 For then shalt thou have thy delight in the Almighty, and shalt lift up thy face unto God.

27 Thou shalt make thy prayer unto him, and he shall hear thee, and thou shalt pay thy vows.

28 Thou shalt also decree a thing, and it shall be established unto thee: and the light shall shine upon thy ways.

Job 27:13-17

13 This is the portion of a wicked man with God, and the heritage of oppressors, which they shall receive of the Almighty.

14 If his children be multiplied, it is for the sword: and his offspring shall not be satisfied with bread.

15 Those that remain of him shall be buried in death: and his widows shall not weep.

16 Though he heap up silver as the dust, and prepare raiment as the clay;

17 He may prepare it, but the just shall put it on, and the innocent shall divide the silver.

Job 42:10, 12

10 And the Lord turned the captivity of Job, when he prayed for his friends: also the Lord gave Job twice as much as he had before.

12 So the Lord blessed the latter end of Job more than his beginning: for he had fourteen thousand sheep, and six thousand camels, and a thousand yoke of oxen, and a thousand she asses.

PSALMS
Psalm 1:1-3

1 Blessed is the man that walketh not in the counsel of the ungodly, nor standeth in the way of sinners, nor sitteth in the seat of the scornful.

2 But his delight is in the law of the Lord; and in his law doth he meditate day and night.

3 And he shall be like a tree planted by the rivers of water, that bringeth forth his fruit in his season; his leaf also shall not wither; and whatsoever he doeth shall prosper.

Psalm 23:1

1 The Lord is my shepherd; I shall not want.

Psalm 34:8-10

8 O taste and see that the Lord is good: blessed is

the man that trusteth in him.

9 O fear the Lord, ye his saints: for there is no want to them that fear him.

10 The young lions do lack, and suffer hunger: but they that seek the Lord shall not want any good thing.

Psalm 35:27-28

27 Let them shout for joy, and be glad, that favour my righteous cause: yea, let them say continually, Let the Lord be magnified, which hath pleasure in the prosperity of his servant.

28 And my tongue shall speak of thy righteousness and of thy praise all the day long.

Psalm 37:3-9

3 Trust in the Lord, and do good; so shalt thou dwell in the land, and verily thou shalt be fed.

4 Delight thyself also in the Lord; and he shall give thee the desires of thine heart.

5 Commit thy way unto the Lord; trust also in him; and he shall bring it to pass.

6 And he shall bring forth thy righteousness as the light, and thy judgment as the noonday.

7 Rest in the Lord, and wait patiently for him: fret not thyself because of him who prospereth in his way, because of the man who bringeth wicked devices to pass.

8 Cease from anger, and forsake wrath: fret not thyself in any wise to do evil.

9 For evildoers shall be cut off: but those that wait upon the Lord, they shall inherit the earth.

Psalm 41:1-3
(To the chief Musician, A Psalm of David.)

1 Blessed is he that considereth the poor: the Lord will deliver him in time of trouble.

2 The Lord will preserve him, and keep him alive; and he shall be blessed upon the earth: and thou wilt not deliver him unto the will of his enemies.

3 The Lord will strengthen him upon the bed of languishing: thou wilt make all his bed in his sickness.

Psalm 68:11, 12, 19

11 The Lord gave the word: great was the company of those that published it.

12 Kings of armies did flee apace: and she that tarried at home divided the spoil.

19 Blessed be the Lord, who daily loadeth us with benefits, even the God of our salvation. Selah.

Psalm 73:23-26

23 Nevertheless I am continually with thee: thou hast holden me by my right hand.

24 Thou shalt guide me with thy counsel, and afterward receive me to glory.

25 Whom have I in heaven but thee? and there is none upon earth that I desire beside thee.

26 My flesh and my heart faileth: but God is the strength of my heart, and my portion for ever.

Psalm 75:6, 7

6 For promotion cometh neither from the east, nor

from the west, nor from the south.

7 But God is the judge: he putteth down one, and setteth up another.

Psalm 84:11, 12

11 For the Lord God is a sun and shield: the Lord will give grace and glory: no good thing will he withhold from them that walk uprightly.

12 O Lord of hosts, blessed is the man that trusteth in thee.

Psalm 91:9-16

9 Because thou hast made the Lord, which is my refuge, even the most High, thy habitation;

10 There shall no evil befall thee, neither shall any plague come nigh thy dwelling.

11 For he shall give his angels charge over thee, to keep thee in all thy ways.

12 They shall bear thee up in their hands, lest thou dash thy foot against a stone.

13 Thou shalt tread upon the lion and adder: the young lion and the dragon shalt thou trample under feet.

14 Because he hath set his love upon me, therefore will I deliver him: I will set him on high, because he hath known my name.

15 He shall call upon me, and I will answer him: I will be with him in trouble; I will deliver him, and honour him.

16 With long life will I satisfy him, and shew him my salvation.

Psalm 103:1-5
(A Psalm of David.)

1 Bless the Lord, O my soul: and all that is within me, bless his holy name.

2 Bless the Lord, O my soul, and forget not all his benefits:

3 Who forgiveth all thine iniquities; who healeth all thy diseases;

4 Who redeemeth thy life from destruction; who crowneth thee with lovingkindness and tender mercies;

5 Who satisfieth thy mouth with good things; so that thy youth is renewed like the eagles.

Psalm 105:37

37 He brought them forth also with silver and gold: and there was not one feeble person among their tribes.

Psalm 112

1 Praise ye the Lord. Blessed is the man that feareth the Lord, that delighteth greatly in his commandments.

2 His seed shall be mighty upon earth: the generation of the upright shall be blessed.

3 Wealth and riches shall be in his house: and his righteousness endureth for ever.

4 Unto the upright there ariseth light in the darkness: he is gracious, and full of compassion, and righteous.

5 A good man sheweth favour, and lendeth: he will

guide his affairs with discretion.

6 Surely he shall not be moved for ever: the righteous shall be in everlasting remembrance.

7 He shall not be afraid of evil tidings: his heart is fixed, trusting in the Lord.

8 His heart is established, he shall not be afraid, until he see his desire upon his enemies.

9 He hath dispersed, he hath given to the poor; his righteousness endureth for ever; his horn shall be exalted with honour.

10 The wicked shall see it, and be grieved; he shall gnash with his teeth, and melt away: the desire of the wicked shall perish.

Psalm 116:12-14

12 What shall I render unto the Lord for all his benefits toward me?

13 I will take the cup of salvation, and call upon the name of the Lord.

14 I will pay my vows unto the Lord now in the presence of all his people.

Psalm 118:8, 9, 25, 26

8 It is better to trust in the Lord than to put confidence in man.

9 It is better to trust in the Lord than to put confidence in princes.

25 Save now, I beseech thee, O Lord: O Lord, I beseech thee, send now prosperity.

26 Blessed be he that cometh in the name of the Lord: we have blessed you out of the house of the Lord.

Psalm 119:165

165 Great peace have they which love thy law: and nothing shall offend them.

Psalm 132:13-16

13 For the Lord hath chosen Zion; he hath desired it for his habitation.

14 This is my rest for ever: here will I dwell; for I have desired it.

15 I will abundantly bless her provision: I will satisfy her poor with bread.

16 I will also clothe her priests with salvation: and her saints shall shout aloud for joy.

Psalm 136:23-25

23 Who remembered us in our low estate: for his mercy endureth for ever:

24 And hath redeemed us from our enemies: for his mercy endureth for ever.

25 Who giveth food to all flesh: for his mercy endureth for ever.

Psalm 138:7, 8

7 Though I walk in the midst of trouble, thou wilt revive me: thou shalt stretch forth thine hand against the wrath of mine enemies, and thy right hand shall save me.

8 The Lord will perfect that which concerneth me: thy mercy, O Lord, endureth for ever: forsake not the works of thine own hands.

Psalm 145:18, 19

18 The Lord is nigh unto all them that call upon him, to all that call upon him in truth.

19 He will fulfil the desire of them that fear him: he also will hear their cry, and will save them.

PROVERBS
Proverbs 3:1, 2, 9, 10, 13-17, 27, 28

1 My son, forget not my law; but let thine heart keep my commandments:

2 For length of days, and long life, and peace, shall they add to thee.

9 Honour the Lord with thy substance, and with the firstfruits of all thine increase:

10 So shall thy barns be filled with plenty, and thy presses shall burst out with new wine.

13 Happy is the man that findeth wisdom, and the man that getteth understanding.

14 For the merchandise of it is better than the merchandise of silver, and the gain thereof than fine gold.

15 She is more precious than rubies: and all the things thou canst desire are not to be compared unto her.

16 Length of days is in her right hand; and in her left hand riches and honour.

17 Her ways are ways of pleasantness, and all her paths are peace.

27 Withhold not good from them to whom it is due, when it is in the power of thine hand to do it.

28 Say not unto thy neighbour, Go, and come again, and tomorrow I will give; when thou hast it by thee.

Proverbs 8:17-21

17 I love them that love me; and those that seek me early shall find me.

18 Riches and honour are with me; yea, durable riches and righteousness.

19 My fruit is better than gold, yea, than fine gold; and my revenue than choice silver.

20 I lead in the way of righteousness, in the midst of the paths of judgment:

21 That I may cause those that love me to inherit substance; and I will fill their treasures.

Proverbs 10:3, 4, 22-24

3 The Lord will not suffer the soul of the righteous to famish: but he casteth away the substance of the wicked.

4 He becometh poor that dealeth with a slack hand: but the hand of the diligent maketh rich.

22 The blessing of the Lord, it maketh rich, and he addeth no sorrow with it.

23 It is as sport to a fool to do mischief: but a man of understanding hath wisdom.

24 The fear of the wicked, it shall come upon him: but the desire of the righteous shall be granted.

Proverbs 11:24-28

24 There is that scattereth, and yet increaseth; and there is that withholdeth more than is meet, but it tendeth to poverty.

25 The liberal soul shall be made fat: and he that watereth shall be watered also himself.

26 He that withholdeth corn, the people shall curse him: but blessing shall be upon the head of him that selleth it.

27 He that diligently seeketh good procureth favour: but he that seeketh mischief, it shall come unto him.

28 He that trusteth in his riches shall fall: but the righteous shall flourish as a branch.

Proverbs 13:4, 11, 18, 21-25

4 The soul of the sluggard desireth, and hath nothing: but the soul of the diligent shall be made fat.

11 Wealth gotten by vanity shall be diminished: but he that gathereth by labour shall increase.

18 Poverty and shame shall be to him that refuseth instruction: but he that regardeth reproof shall be honoured.

21 Evil pursueth sinners: but to the righteous good shall be repaid.

22 A good man leaveth an inheritance to his children's children: and the wealth of the sinner is laid up for the just.

23 Much food is in the tillage of the poor: but there is that is destroyed for want of judgment.

24 He that spareth his rod hateth his son: but he that loveth him chasteneth him betimes.

25 The righteous eateth to the satisfying of his soul: but the belly of the wicked shall want.

Proverbs 15:6

6 In the house of the righteous is much treasure:

but in the revenues of the wicked is trouble.

Proverbs 18:20

20 A man's belly shall be satisfied with the fruit of his mouth; and with the increase of his lips shall he be filled.

Proverbs 19:17

17 He that hath pity upon the poor lendeth unto the Lord; and that which he hath given will he pay him again.

Proverbs 22:1-4, 9, 29

1 A good name is rather to be chosen than great riches, and loving favour rather than silver and gold.

2 The rich and poor meet together: the Lord is the maker of them all.

3 A prudent man foreseeth the evil, and hideth himself: but the simple pass on, and are punished.

4 By humility and the fear of the Lord are riches, and honour, and life.

9 He that hath a bountiful eye shall be blessed; for he giveth of his bread to the poor.

29 Seest thou a man diligent in his business? he shall stand before kings; he shall not stand before mean men.

Proverbs 24:3, 4, 30-34

3 Through wisdom is an house builded; and by understanding it is established:

4 And by knowledge shall the chambers be filled with all precious and pleasant riches.

30 I went by the field of the slothful, and by the vineyard of the man void of understanding;

31 And, lo, it was all grown over with thorns, and nettles had covered the face thereof, and the stone wall thereof was broken down.

32 Then I saw, and considered it well: I looked upon it, and received instruction.

33 Yet a little sleep, a little slumber, a little folding of the hands to sleep:

34 So shall thy poverty come as one that travelleth; and thy want as an armed man.

Proverbs 28:19, 20, 27

19 He that tilleth his land shall have plenty of bread: but he that followeth after vain persons shall have poverty enough.

20 A faithful man shall abound with blessings: but he that maketh haste to be rich shall not be innocent.

27 He that giveth unto the poor shall not lack: but he that hideth his eyes shall have many a curse.

ECCLESIASTES
Ecclesiastes 2:26

26 For God giveth to a man that is good in his sight wisdom, and knowledge, and joy: but to the sinner he giveth travail, to gather and to heap up, that he may give to him that is good before God. This also is vanity and vexation of spirit.

Ecclesiastes 3:1, 2

1 To every thing there is a season, and a time to

every purpose under the heaven:

2 A time to be born, and a time to die; a time to plant, and a time to pluck up that which is planted;

Ecclesiastes 5:10-13, 18-20

10 He that loveth silver shall not be satisfied with silver; nor he that loveth abundance with increase: this is also vanity.

11 When goods increase, they are increased that eat them: and what good is there to the owners thereof, saving the beholding of them with their eyes?

12 The sleep of a labouring man is sweet, whether he eat little or much: but the abundance of the rich will not suffer him to sleep.

13 There is a sore evil which I have seen under the sun, namely, riches kept for the owners thereof to their hurt.

18 Behold that which I have seen: it is good and comely for one to eat and to drink, and to enjoy the good of all his labour that he taketh under the sun all the days of his life, which God giveth him: for it is his portion.

19 Every man also to whom God hath given riches and wealth, and hath given him power to eat thereof, and to take his portion, and to rejoice in his labour; this is the gift of God.

20 For he shall not much remember the days of his life; because God answereth him in the joy of his heart.

SONG OF SOLOMON
Song of Solomon 2:4
4 He brought me to the banqueting house, and his banner over me was love.

ISAIAH
Isaiah 45:2, 3
2 I will go before thee, and make the crooked places straight: I will break in pieces the gates of brass, and cut in sunder the bars of iron:

3 And I will give thee the treasures of darkness, and hidden riches of secret places, that thou mayest know that I, the Lord, which call thee by thy name, am the God of Israel.

Isaiah 48:17-18
17 Thus saith the Lord, thy Redeemer, the Holy One of Israel; I am the Lord thy God which teacheth thee to profit, which leadeth thee by the way that thou shouldest go.

18 O that thou hadst hearkened to my commandments then had thy peace been as a river, and thy righteousness as the waves of the sea:

Isaiah 55:10, 11
10 For as the rain cometh down, and the snow from heaven, and returneth not thither, but watereth the earth, and maketh it bring forth and bud, that it may give seed to the sower, and bread to the eater:

11 So shall my word be that goeth forth out of my mouth: it shall not return unto me void, but it shall accomplish that which I please, and it shall prosper in the thing whereto I sent it.

Isaiah 60:5, 6

5 Then thou shalt see, and flow together, and thine heart shall fear, and be enlarged; because the abundance of the sea shall be converted unto thee, the forces of the Gentiles shall come unto thee.

6 The multitude of camels shall cover thee, the dromedaries of Midian and Ephah; all they from Sheba shall come: they shall bring gold and incense; and they shall shew forth the praises of the Lord.

Isaiah 61:6

6 But ye shall be named the Priests of the Lord: men shall call you the Ministers of our God: ye shall eat the riches of the Gentiles, and in their glory shall ye boast yourselves.

JEREMIAH
Jeremiah 17:7, 8

7 Blessed is the man that trusteth in the Lord, and whose hope the Lord is.

8 For he shall be as a tree planted by the waters, and that spreadeth out her roots by the river, and shall not see when heat cometh, but her leaf shall be green; and shall not be careful in the year of drought, neither shall cease from yielding fruit.

Jeremiah 29:11, 12

11 For I know the thoughts that I think toward you, saith the Lord, thoughts of peace, and not of evil, to give you an expected end.

12 Then shall ye call upon me, and ye shall go and pray unto me, and I will hearken unto you.

Jeremiah 30:16

16 Therefore all they that devour thee shall be devoured; and all thine adversaries, every one of them, shall go into captivity; and they that spoil thee shall be a spoil, and all that prey upon thee will I give for a prey.

Jeremiah 31:16, 17

16 Thus saith the Lord; Refrain thy voice from weeping, and thine eyes from tears: for thy work shall be rewarded, saith the Lord; and they shall come again from the land of the enemy.

17 And there is hope in thine end, saith the Lord, that thy children shall come again to their own border.

LAMENTATIONS
Lamentations 3:22-33

22 It is of the Lord's mercies that we are not consumed, because his compassions fail not.

23 They are new every morning: great is thy faithfulness.

24 The Lord is my portion, saith my soul; therefore will I hope in him.

25 The Lord is good unto them that wait for him, to the soul that seeketh him.

26 It is good that a man should both hope and quietly wait for the salvation of the Lord.

27 It is good for a man that he bear the yoke in his youth.

28 He sitteth alone and keepeth silence, because he hath borne it upon him.

29 He putteth his mouth in the dust; if so be there may be hope.

30 He giveth his cheek to him that smiteth him: he is filled full with reproach.

31 For the Lord will not cast off for ever:

32 But though he cause grief, yet will he have compassion according to the multitude of his mercies.

33 For he doth not afflict willingly, nor grieve the children of men.

EZEKIEL
Ezekiel 36:26-30

26 A new heart also will I give you, and a new spirit will I put within you: and I will take away the stony heart out of your flesh, and I will give you an heart of flesh.

27 And I will put my spirit within you, and cause you to walk in my statutes, and ye shall keep my judgments, and do them.

28 And ye shall dwell in the land that I gave to your fathers; and ye shall be my people, and I will be your God.

29 I will also save you from all your uncleannesses: and I will call for the corn, and will increase it, and lay no famine upon you.

30 And I will multiply the fruit of the tree, and the increase of the field, that ye shall receive no more reproach of famine among the heathen.

Ezekiel 47:9

9 And it shall come to pass, that every thing that liveth, which moveth, whithersoever the rivers shall come, shall live: and there shall be a very great multitude of fish, because these waters shall come thither: for they shall be healed; and every thing shall live whither the river cometh.

DANIEL
Daniel 11:32b

32b the people that do know their God shall be strong, and do exploits.

HOSEA
Hosea 6:1-3

1 Come, and let us return unto the Lord: for he hath torn, and he will heal us; he hath smitten, and he will bind us up.

2 After two days will he revive us: in the third day he will raise us up, and we shall live in his sight.

3 Then shall we know, if we follow on to know the Lord: his going forth is prepared as the morning; and he shall come unto us as the rain, as the latter and former rain unto the earth.

JOEL
Joel 2:23-26

23 Be glad then, ye children of Zion, and rejoice in the Lord your God: for he hath given you the former rain moderately, and he will cause to come down for you the rain, the former rain, and the latter rain in the first month.

24 And the floors shall be full of wheat, and the vats shall overflow with wine and oil.

25 And I will restore to you the years that the locust hath eaten, the cankerworm, and the caterpillar, and the palmerworm, my great army which I sent among you.

26 And ye shall eat in plenty, and be satisfied, and praise the name of the Lord your God, that hath dealt wondrously with you: and my people shall never be ashamed.

AMOS
Amos 5:4

4 For thus saith the Lord unto the house of Israel, Seek ye me, and ye shall live:

Amos 9:5, 6, 13, 14

5 And the Lord God of hosts is he that toucheth the land, and it shall melt, and all that dwell therein shall mourn: and it shall rise up wholly like a flood; and shall be drowned, as by the flood of Egypt.

6 It is he that buildeth his stories in the heaven, and hath founded his troop in the earth; he that calleth for the waters of the sea, and poureth them out

upon the face of the earth: The Lord is his name.

13 Behold, the days come, saith the Lord, that the plowman shall overtake the reaper, and the treader of grapes him that soweth seed; and the mountains shall drop sweet wine, and all the hills shall melt.

14 And I will bring again the captivity of my people of Israel, and they shall build the waste cities, and inhabit them; and they shall plant vineyards, and drink the wine thereof; they shall also make gardens, and eat the fruit of them.

OBADIAH
Obadiah 1:17

17 But upon mount Zion shall be deliverance, and there shall be holiness; and the house of Jacob shall possess their possessions.

JONAH
Jonah 2:2

2 And said, I cried by reason of mine affliction unto the Lord, and he heard me; out of the belly of hell cried I, and thou heardest my voice.

MICAH
Micah 6:8

8 He hath shewed thee, O man, what is good; and what doth the Lord require of thee, but to do justly, and to love mercy, and to walk humbly with thy God?

NAHUM
Nahum 1:13

13 For now will I break his yoke from off thee, and will burst thy bonds in sunder.

HABAKKUK
Habakkuk 2:3

3 For the vision is yet for an appointed time, but at the end it shall speak, and not lie: though it tarry, wait for it; because it will surely come, it will not tarry.

ZEPHANIAH
Zephaniah 3:17

17 The Lord thy God in the midst of thee is mighty; he will save, he will rejoice over thee with joy; he will rest in his love, he will joy over thee with singing.

HAGGAI
Haggai 2:8, 9

8 The silver is mine, and the gold is mine, saith the Lord of hosts.

9 The glory of this latter house shall be greater than of the former, saith the Lord of hosts: and in this place will I give peace, saith the Lord of hosts.

ZECHARIAH
Zechariah 8:12, 13

12 For the seed shall be prosperous; the vine shall give her fruit, and the ground shall give her

increase, and the heavens shall give their dew; and I will cause the remnant of this people to possess all these things.

13 And it shall come to pass, that as ye were a curse among the heathen, O house of Judah, and house of Israel; so will I save you, and ye shall be a blessing: fear not, but let your hands be strong.

MALACHI
Malachi 3:10-12

10 Bring ye all the tithes into the storehouse, that there may be meat in mine house, and prove me now herewith, saith the Lord of hosts, if I will not open you the windows of heaven, and pour you out a blessing, that there shall not be room enough to receive it.

11 And I will rebuke the devourer for your sakes, and he shall not destroy the fruits of your ground; neither shall your vine cast her fruit before the time in the field, saith the Lord of hosts.

12 And all nations shall call you blessed: for ye shall be a delightsome land, saith the Lord of hosts.

MATTHEW
Matthew 6:19-34

19 Lay not up for yourselves treasures upon earth, where moth and rust doth corrupt, and where thieves break through and steal:

20 But lay up for yourselves treasures in heaven, where neither moth nor rust doth corrupt, and where thieves do not break through nor steal:

21 For where your treasure is, there will your heart be also.

22 The light of the body is the eye: if therefore thine eye be single, thy whole body shall be full of light.

23 But if thine eye be evil, thy whole body shall be full of darkness. If therefore the light that is in thee be darkness, how great is that darkness

24 No man can serve two masters: for either he will hate the one, and love the other; or else he will hold to the one, and despise the other. Ye cannot serve God and mammon.

25 Therefore I say unto you, Take no thought for your life, what ye shall eat, or what ye shall drink; nor yet for your body, what ye shall put on. Is not the life more than meat, and the body than raiment?

26 Behold the fowls of the air: for they sow not, neither do they reap, nor gather into barns; yet your heavenly Father feedeth them. Are ye not much better than they?

27 Which of you by taking thought can add one cubit unto his stature?

28 And why take ye thought for raiment? Consider the lilies of the field, how they grow; they toil not, neither do they spin:

29 And yet I say unto you, That even Solomon in all his glory was not arrayed like one of these.

30 Wherefore, if God so clothe the grass of the field, which today is, and tomorrow is cast into the oven, shall he not much more clothe you, O ye of little faith?

31 Therefore take no thought, saying, What shall we eat? or, What shall we drink? or, Wherewithal shall we be clothed?

32 (For after all these things do the Gentiles seek:) for your heavenly Father knoweth that ye have need of all these things.

33 But seek ye first the kingdom of God, and his righteousness; and all these things shall be added unto you.

34 Take therefore no thought for the morrow: for the morrow shall take thought for the things of itself. Sufficient unto the day is the evil thereof.

MARK
Mark 10:17-31

17 And when he was gone forth into the way, there came one running, and kneeled to him, and asked him, Good Master, what shall I do that I may inherit eternal life?

18 And Jesus said unto him, Why callest thou me good? there is none good but one, that is, God.

19 Thou knowest the commandments, Do not commit adultery, Do not kill, Do not steal, Do not bear false witness, Defraud not, Honour thy father and mother.

20 And he answered and said unto him, Master, all these have I observed from my youth.

21 Then Jesus beholding him loved him, and said unto him, One thing thou lackest: go thy way, sell whatsoever thou hast, and give to the poor, and thou

shalt have treasure in heaven: and come, take up the cross, and follow me.

22 And he was sad at that saying, and went away grieved: for he had great possessions.

23 And Jesus looked round about, and saith unto his disciples, How hardly shall they that have riches enter into the kingdom of God!

24 And the disciples were astonished at his words. But Jesus answereth again, and saith unto them, Children, how hard is it for them that trust in riches to enter into the kingdom of God!

25 It is easier for a camel to go through the eye of a needle, than for a rich man to enter into the kingdom of God.

26 And they were astonished out of measure, saying among themselves, Who then can be saved?

27 And Jesus looking upon them saith, With men it is impossible, but not with God: for with God all things are possible.

28 Then Peter began to say unto him, Lo, we have left all, and have followed thee.

29 And Jesus answered and said, Verily I say unto you, There is no man that hath left house, or brethren, or sisters, or father, or mother, or wife, or children, or lands, for my sake, and the gospels,

30 But he shall receive an hundredfold now in this time, houses, and brethren, and sisters, and mothers, and children, and lands, with persecutions; and in the world to come eternal life.

31 But many that are first shall be last; and the last first.

LUKE
Luke 6:38

38 Give, and it shall be given unto you; good measure, pressed down, and shaken together, and running over, shall men give into your bosom. For with the same measure that ye mete withal it shall be measured to you again.

JOHN
John 14:2, 3, 12-14, 27, 28

2 In my Father's house are many mansions: if it were not so, I would have told you. I go to prepare a place for you.

3 And if I go and prepare a place for you, I will come again, and receive you unto myself; that where I am, there ye may be also.

12 Verily, verily, I say unto you, He that believeth on me, the works that I do shall he do also; and greater works than these shall he do; because I go unto my Father.

13 And whatsoever ye shall ask in my name, that will I do, that the Father may be glorified in the Son.

14 If ye shall ask any thing in my name, I will do it.

27 Peace I leave with you, my peace I give unto you: not as the world giveth, give I unto you. Let not your heart be troubled, neither let it be afraid.

28 Ye have heard how I said unto you, I go away, and come again unto you, If ye loved me, ye would rejoice, because I said, I go unto the Father: for my Father is greater than I.

ACTS
Acts 4:33-35

33 And with great power gave the apostles witness of the resurrection of the Lord Jesus: and great grace was upon them all.

34 Neither was there any among them that lacked: for as many as were possessors of lands or houses sold them, and brought the prices of the things that were sold,

35 And laid them down at the apostles feet: and distribution was made unto every man according as he had need.

ROMANS
Romans 8:28, 32, 35-39

28 And we know that all things work together for good to them that love God, to them who are the called according to his purpose.

32 He that spared not his own Son, but delivered him up for us all, how shall he not with him also freely give us all things?

35 Who shall separate us from the love of Christ? shall tribulation, or distress, or persecution, or famine, or nakedness, or peril, or sword?

36 As it is written, For thy sake we are killed all the day long; we are accounted as sheep for the slaughter.

37 Nay, in all these things we are more than conquerors through him that loved us.

38 For I am persuaded, that neither death, nor life, nor angels, nor principalities, nor powers, nor things

present, nor things to come,

39 Nor height, nor depth, nor any other creature, shall be able to separate us from the love of God, which is in Christ Jesus our Lord.

Romans 11:33-36

33 O the depth of the riches both of the wisdom and knowledge of God how unsearchable are his judgments, and his ways past finding out!

34 For who hath known the mind of the Lord? or who hath been his counsellor?

35 Or who hath first given to him, and it shall be recompensed unto him again?

36 For of him, and through him, and to him, are all things: to whom be glory for ever. Amen.

Romans 13:8

8 Owe no man any thing, but to love one another: for he that loveth another hath fulfilled the law.

1 CORINTHIANS
1 Corinthians 4:2

2 Moreover it is required in stewards, that a man be found faithful.

2 CORINTHIANS
2 Corinthians 8:1-15

1 Moreover, brethren, we do you to wit of the grace of God bestowed on the churches of Macedonia;

2 How that in a great trial of affliction the abundance of their joy and their deep poverty abounded unto the riches of their liberality.

3 For to their power, I bear record, yea, and beyond their power they were willing of themselves;

4 Praying us with much entreaty that we would receive the gift, and take upon us the fellowship of the ministering to the saints.

5 And this they did, not as we hoped, but first gave their own selves to the Lord, and unto us by the will of God.

6 Insomuch that we desired Titus, that as he had begun, so he would also finish in you the same grace also.

7 Therefore, as ye abound in every thing, in faith, and utterance, and knowledge, and in all diligence, and in your love to us, see that ye abound in this grace also.

8 I speak not by commandment, but by occasion of the forwardness of others, and to prove the sincerity of your love.

9 For ye know the grace of our Lord Jesus Christ, that, though he was rich, yet for your sakes he became poor, that ye through his poverty might be rich.

10 And herein I give my advice: for this is expedient for you, who have begun before, not only to do, but also to be forward a year ago.

11 Now therefore perform the doing of it; that as there was a readiness to will, so there may be a performance also out of that which ye have.

12 For if there be first a willing mind, it is accept-ed according to that a man hath, and not according to that he hath not.

13 For I mean not that other men be eased, and ye burdened:

14 But by an equality, that now at this time your abundance may be a supply for their want, that their abundance also may be a supply for your want: that there may be equality:

15 As it is written, He that had gathered much had nothing over; and he that had gathered little had no lack.

2 Corinthians 9:6-11

6 But this I say, He which soweth sparingly shall reap also sparingly; and he which soweth bountifully shall reap also bountifully.

7 Every man according as he purposeth in his heart, so let him give; not grudgingly, or of necessity: for God loveth a cheerful giver.

8 And God is able to make all grace abound toward you; that ye, always having all sufficiency in all things, may abound to every good work:

9 (As it is written, He hath dispersed abroad; he hath given to the poor: his righteousness remaineth for ever.

10 Now he that ministereth seed to the sower both minister bread for your food, and multiply your seed sown, and increase the fruits of your righteousness;)

11 Being enriched in every thing to all bountiful-ness, which causeth through us thanksgiving to God.

GALATIANS
Galatians 3:13

13 Christ hath redeemed us from the curse of the law, being made a curse for us: for it is written, Cursed is every one that hangeth on a tree:

Galatians 6:6-10

6 Let him that is taught in the word communicate unto him that teacheth in all good things.

7 Be not deceived; God is not mocked: for whatsoever a man soweth, that shall he also reap.

8 For he that soweth to his flesh shall of the flesh reap corruption; but he that soweth to the Spirit shall of the Spirit reap life everlasting.

9 And let us not be weary in well doing: for in due season we shall reap, if we faint not.

10 As we have therefore opportunity, let us do good unto all men, especially unto them who are of the household of faith.

EPHESIANS
Ephesians 1:3

3 Blessed be the God and Father of our Lord Jesus Christ, who hath blessed us with all spiritual blessings in heavenly places in Christ:

Ephesians 6:2, 3

2 Honour thy father and mother; which is the first commandment with promise;

3 That it may be well with thee, and thou mayest live long on the earth.

PHILIPPIANS
Philippians 4:6, 13, 19

6 Be careful for nothing; but in every thing by prayer and supplication with thanksgiving let your requests be made known unto God.

13 I can do all things through Christ which strengtheneth me.

19 But my God shall supply all your need according to his riches in glory by Christ Jesus.

COLOSSIANS
Colossians 3:1, 2

1 If ye then be risen with Christ, seek those things which are above, where Christ sitteth on the right hand of God.

2 Set your affection on things above, not on things on the earth.

1 THESSALONIANS
1 Thessalonians 5:12, 13

12 And we beseech you, brethren, to know them which labour among you, and are over you in the Lord, and admonish you;

13 And to esteem them very highly in love for their work's sake. And be at peace among yourselves.

2 THESSALONIANS
2 Thessalonians 3:3

3 But the Lord is faithful, who shall stablish you, and keep you from evil.

1 TIMOTHY

1 Timothy 5:8

8 But if any provide not for his own, and specially for those of his own house, he hath denied the faith, and is worse than an infidel.

1 Timothy 6:7-12, 17-19

7 For we brought nothing into this world, and it is certain we can carry nothing out.

8 And having food and raiment, let us be therewith content.

9 But they that will be rich fall into temptation and a snare, and into many foolish and hurtful lusts, which drown men in destruction and perdition.

10 For the love of money is the root of all evil: which while some coveted after, they have erred from the faith, and pierced themselves through with many sorrows.

11 But thou, O man of God, flee these things; and follow after righteousness, godliness, faith, love, patience, meekness.

12 Fight the good fight of faith, lay hold on eternal life, whereunto thou art also called, and hast professed a good profession before many witnesses.

17 Charge them that are rich in this world, that they be not highminded, nor trust in uncertain riches, but in the living God, who giveth us richly all things to enjoy;

18 That they do good, that they be rich in good works, ready to distribute, willing to communicate;

19 Laying up in store for themselves a good foun-

dation against the time to come, that they may lay hold on eternal life.

2 TIMOTHY
2 Timothy 2:20, 21
20 But in a great house there are not only vessels of gold and of silver, but also of wood and of earth; and some to honour, and some to dishonour.

21 If a man therefore purge himself from these, he shall be a vessel unto honour, sanctified, and meet for the master's use, and prepared unto every good work.

TITUS
Titus 2:12
12 Teaching us that, denying ungodliness and worldly lusts, we should live soberly, righteously, and godly, in this present world;

PHILEMON
Philemon 1:6
6 That the communication of thy faith may become effectual by the acknowledging of every good thing which is in you in Christ Jesus.

HEBREWS
Hebrews 11:1
1 Now faith is the substance of things hoped for, the evidence of things not seen.

Hebrews 13:15, 16, 20, 21

15 By him therefore let us offer the sacrifice of praise to God continually, that is, the fruit of our lips, giving thanks to his name.

16 But to do good and to communicate forget not: for with such sacrifices God is well pleased.

20 Now the God of peace, that brought again from the dead our Lord Jesus, that great shepherd of the sheep, through the blood of the everlasting covenant,

21 Make you perfect in every good work to do his will, working in you that which is wellpleasing in his sight, through Jesus Christ; to whom be glory for ever and ever. Amen.

JAMES
James 1:17

17 Every good gift and every perfect gift is from above, and cometh down from the Father of lights, with whom is no variableness, neither shadow of turning.

1 PETER
1 Peter 2:9

9 But ye are a chosen generation, a royal priesthood, an holy nation, a peculiar people; that ye should shew forth the praises of him who hath called you out of darkness into his marvellous light:

1 Peter 3:12, 13

12 For the eyes of the Lord are over the righteous, and his ears are open unto their prayers: but the face of

the Lord is against them that do evil.

13 And who is he that will harm you, if ye be followers of that which is good?

2 PETER
2 Peter 1:3
3 According as his divine power hath given unto us all things that pertain unto life and godliness, through the knowledge of him that hath called us to glory and virtue:

1 JOHN
1 John 3:22
22 And whatsoever we ask, we receive of him, because we keep his commandments, and do those things that are pleasing in his sight.

1 John 5:14, 15
14 And this is the confidence that we have in him, that, if we ask any thing according to his will, he heareth us:

15 And if we know that he hear us, whatsoever we ask, we know that we have the petitions that we desired of him.

2 JOHN
2 John 1:4-6
4 I rejoiced greatly that I found of thy children walking in truth, as we have received a commandment from the Father.

5 And now I beseech thee, lady, not as though I wrote a new commandment unto thee, but that which we had from the beginning, that we love one another.

6 And this is love, that we walk after his commandments. This is the commandment, That, as ye have heard from the beginning, ye should walk in it.

3 JOHN
3 John 1:2

2 Beloved, I wish above all things that thou mayest prosper and be in health, even as thy soul prospereth.

JUDE
Jude 1:20, 21

20 But ye, beloved, building up yourselves on your most holy faith, praying in the Holy Ghost,

21 Keep yourselves in the love of God, looking for the mercy of our Lord Jesus Christ unto eternal life.

REVELATION
Revelation 21:1-7

1 And I saw a new heaven and a new earth: for the first heaven and the first earth were passed away; and there was no more sea.

2 And I John saw the holy city, new Jerusalem, coming down from God out of heaven, prepared as a bride adorned for her husband.

3 And I heard a great voice out of heaven saying, Behold, the tabernacle of God is with men, and he will

dwell with them, and they shall be his people, and God himself shall be with them, and be their God.

4 And God shall wipe away all tears from their eyes; and there shall be no more death, neither sorrow, nor crying, neither shall there be any more pain: for the former things are passed away.

5 And he that sat upon the throne said, Behold, I make all things new. And he said unto me, Write: for these words are true and faithful.

6 And he said unto me, It is done. I am Alpha and Omega, the beginning and the end. I will give unto him that is athirst of the fountain of the water of life freely.

7 He that overcometh shall inherit all things; and I will be his God, and he shall be my son.